AMAZING CATS

CUTE CATS FROM DIFFERENT WORLD PLACE COLORING BOOK

HTTPS://WWW.INSTAGRAM.COM/RIMMA.FOX.ART

MAGIC CAT

SIBERIAN CAT

SPHYNX CAT

ORIENTAL SHORTHAIR

PERSIAN CAT

CHRISTMAS CAT

CAT STORYTELLER

CORNISH REX

AUTUMN CAT

BRITISH SHORTHAIR

BURMESE CAT

BIRMAN

ABYSSINIAN CAT

AMERICAN SHORTHAIR

MAiNE COON

CAT SAILOR

COUNTRY CAT

SIAMESE CAT

WITCH CAT

TRICOLOR CAT